WALKING WITH GOD

John Birch

DEDICATION

For the many who have offered encouragement.

Table of Contents

ACKNOWLEDGMENTS

Thanks to the many who follow my daily postings on the Faith and Worship Facebook page, as this is the main source for the contents of this book, and the daily encouragement to take time out early in the morning and concentrate on nothing more than a single prayer thought. That's the intention anyway, and I confess some days are better than others!

At the Start of the Day

For this new morning;
its joys and sorrows,
highs and lows,
triumphs and failures,
laughter and pain.
But more than this;
your presence with us,
grace and peace,
wholeness, freedom
to speak your name.
For this new morning
we give you thanks.

This day, Lord
is our offering.
May the words
we speak bring
only blessing,
and our hearts
reflect your grace.

This is your day, Lord,
and through its joys,
struggles and issues
we shall endeavour
to be your servants,
and whatever we do
or say, be informed
by the love you show
and the grace we know
daily in our walk of faith.

I commit this day
into your hands.
Loving hands,
caring hands,
guiding hands,
healing hands,
guarding hands,
forgiving hands.
Into your hands
I commit this day.

As this week's journey begins,
in the company of others,
but more importantly, with you,
there is one thing I would pray,
that in all things it might be
your will, not mine, that is done
in this world, and my life, today.

At the beginning of this day
walk confidently with God,
knowing his love within you,
his peace surrounding you
and his supporting strength
guarding and guiding you
on your journey of faith today.

May the Good Shepherd
keep you safe today.
May you be nourished
by the Word of Life.
May you be refreshed
by streams of water.
May you be sheltered
and free from harm.
May you be kept warm
through the coldest night.
And may you follow,
in confidence and trust,
where the Good Shepherd
in his wisdom leads you.

Merciful God,
may the choices
I make today
be wise ones,
for the good
of everybody,
and not just me.

Guide us safely through this day,
and at its end, grant us sweet rest.

Nine to Five

Walk beside us today,
and open our eyes
to opportunities
where a smile,
a word, a hug,
a few moments
from our busyness,
shared along the way,
might help someone
who is struggling
on their own walk today.

Knowing you are with us
in the ebbs and flows
of our everyday lives,
your Spirit's presence
within our hearts,
your gentle whisper
guiding our steps,
your warm embrace
when times are hard,
your hands held out
each time we fall.
Knowing you are with us
in our everyday lives
is blessing enough for today.

Be the peace that calms
the stress within this day,
that gentle whisper, yet
louder than the world,
'Be still, breathe deeply,
let my Spirit fill your soul.'

However busy I might be,
may there be moments
when I am alone, to think,
to pray, to hear your voice
and know your presence
within and beside me,
through this and every day.

Be the light we walk by
Be the peace we know
Be the truth we hold to
Be the love we show.

May you know God's peace
within the storms of life;
and in the quietness beyond,
as the waves subside,
hear that gentle whisper,
'Be still, my child, and rest.'

Within the clutter
and confusion
of our daily lives
help us prioritise,
be good stewards
of our time and love,
grateful servants
of our gracious God.

Put a song in our hearts,
one that the angels sing,
and throughout our lives
your praise will ring.

God's word direct you
God's grace inspire you
God's love shine from you
God's peace surround you
God's strength protect you
through this and every day

Purify our hearts
and minds,
that our worship
and lives
might glorify you.

May your kingdom's values
be seen within our hearts,
find expression in our lives
and transform this world,
by the power of your Spirit
living in and through us.

Breath of God
blow the dust
from this life,
all that dulls
the brightness
of your radiance,
that it might shine
again as new.

You are the whisper in the breeze,
calm voice within each storm,
the lamp inside my darkness
and guidance along this road.
You are the hidden treasure.
You are the pearl of great price.
You are the one who occupies
the God-shaped hole within my life
that no other can ever fill.

Loving God, take my life,
this work-in-progress,
getting-there-slowly,
holding-on-tightly life
and, one step at a time
build up my confidence,
so I might simply let go,
and become the person
you've waited patiently,
and with love, for me to be.

God bless your conversations,
wherever they take place.
May your words bring wisdom,
compassion, comfort, peace,
encouragement, change
into someone's life today.
And in the blessing given
may your life also be blessed.

Attune our ears to hear
your gentle whisper,
through every moment
of this precious day.

You are the voice of calm,
the quiet whisper heard
within a stress-filled day.
You are a healing balm
deep in our aching hearts
that takes the pain away.

Lighten the dark
corners, clear
away the debris,
refresh, renew,
and let this life
be lived for you.

Open our eyes to see
the world as you see it.
Open our ears to hear
the world as you hear it.
Open our hearts to love
the world as you love it.

The word of God
become your daily guide.
The light of Christ
illuminate your way.
The Holy Spirit
warm both heart and soul.
The Three in One
be with you every day.

Holy Spirit, gentle river,
irrigate this heart,
that it might truly
live and love and grow.

Eternal flame
burn brightly
in my heart,
and your light
be revealed
as it is opened.

God's Word informing you,
God's peace encircling you,
God's Spirit upholding you,
God's love defining you,
go gently into the world,
becoming the difference
so many are searching for
and have yet to find.

God's arms warm you
on the coldest day,
God's hand guide you
when you lose your way,
God's joy fill you
with a song to sing,
God's love for you
become your offering.

You are my fortress
and strong defence,
protecting me daily.
You are my strength
and also my refuge,
so I will praise you.

Be in the work we do today,
in the simplest of tasks
or in complex decisions.
May your love shine through
in our attitude and actions,
and become a blessing to others.

Let your love shine through
whatever this day brings,
hearts be opened, lives
transformed, and above all
your name be glorified.

Break the chains that constrain us,
and by your Spirit release us.

May you know quietness
within your daily life,
in those moments
of stillness hearing echoes
of the angels' song;
'Holy, holy, holy
is the Lord God almighty
who was, and is,
and is to come'.
May you, with heart and soul,
join in their worship.

As this day begins
refocus our vision
away from self,
that small place
we inhabit,
to the beauty
that surrounds us
in places, faces,
birdsong, laughter,
acts of kindness,
generosity,
being thankful
in life and thought.

(Philippians 4:8)

For ears that hear,
mouths that speak,
hands that serve,
hearts that yearn
to walk with you
along life's road,
hear your voice
and do your will,
this, O God, we pray.

Awesome God, in your power
weakness becomes strength;
so fill us, at the start of this day,
that we might have confidence
to share our faith, speak of you,
become your representatives
in this neighbourhood and town,
urging others to seek your face
and find the peace we know.

Loving God, may there always be,
within our everyday activities,
enough time to read your Word,
listening quietly as it speaks
into our lives, strengthens faith
and challenges us once more
to face each day with confidence,
carrying your light into this world.

Lord, may this be a day
of kind words, listening,
patience, generosity of
time, skill and resource.
Lord, may this be a day
of giving and receiving,
both seeing and feeling
the blessing of your love.
Lord, may this be a day
of comfort and healing,
friendship, truthfulness,
honesty and openness.
Lord, may this be a day
to bring a smile to your face.

Eternal Gardener, make us
as trees planted in fertile soil,
supported, watered and fed
until roots are deep and strong,
trained and pruned if needed
so we might, in due season,
blossom and produce good fruit,
pleasing to your eyes, sweet,
a worthy harvest and offering.

Open our hearts to release
the potential that lies within,
give it wings and let it fly.

Gracious Spirit, be in
the prayers we offer,
that they might not be
simply empty words
drifting heavenward,
but your living breath
changing this world
and these lives together.

Take from us the fear
of words in praying,
and free our voices
to use the language
we comfortably speak
to family, loved ones
and our dearest friends;
that our conversations
might become as natural
as every breath we take.

The whisper of God be your guide
in your journey through this day.
That gentle, persistent reminder
to engage with those around,
offer encouragement, prayer
and support where it is needed,
speak into conversations
both locally and further afield,
give your faith perspective,
and show God's love and peace
when faced with difficult situations.
In your journey through this day
the whisper of God be your guide.

Travelling in Faith

Sometimes small steps
seem like giant leaps
into the unknown
on this journey of faith.
But with you as guide
we need not fear,
for you know the path,
its beautiful views
and hidden dangers,
and you will keep us
out of harm's way
until at last we see
our glorious destination.

We give thanks for Thomas,
who shows us that doubting
is not denying but being honest
both with ourselves and you,
who meets us at those places
where we struggle, opens doors
that seem now to be closed,
and gives us space to recognise
the one who stands before us,
so we can say, with confidence,
'You are my Lord and God'.

You are our
sufficiency
in times of
emptiness.

I rejoice that you accept me
as I am, incomplete, but willing
with your help to become
the person you know I can be.

Creating and loving God
you know the potential
lying within each of us;
unfinished symphonies
waiting to be completed,
clay waiting to be shaped,
and stories yet to unfold.
Open our eyes and hearts
that we might embrace
this vision that you have
of the people we could be,
and give us the courage
to let you begin that work
in our hearts and lives today.

Lord, we are not perfect;
perhaps 'work in progress'
more properly defines us,
as you daily shape the clay
from which we are formed
and gradually transform us.
But deep inside is a heart
that beats to your rhythm,
a soul that seeks the truth.
Despite our imperfections
these lives are lived for you.

In your reading of God's word
may your eyes by opened.
In your listening for God's word
may your ears be opened.
In your obedience to God's word
may your heart be opened,
your life transformed and blessed.

Be my lighthouse in the darkness,
an anchor in the storms,
and lead me back into the harbour
to the safety of your arms.

Gracious God, forgive the me
who tries to override your call
by arguing for a compromise,
an easier, less challenging way.
Forgive the me who hesitates,
puts you on hold for a while,
because I miss the urgency
within your voice, the reason
why, just now, you do need me.

I have lit a candle, Lord,
and in the stillness
within its flame
I glimpse your light.

I have lit a candle, Lord,
and in the stillness
within its warmth
I sense your love.

I have lit a candle, Lord,
and in the stillness
of this moment
I bring my prayer

Heavenly Father
forgive the me
who daily tries
to tug your arm
and take a path
that, to my eyes
seems much easier,
when you know
the one prepared,
which we are on,
has a much more
glorious destination.

Forgive our reluctance
to raise our voices
where we see injustice.
Forgive our reluctance
to become involved
where we see suffering.
Forgive our reluctance
to become a light
in this world's darkness.
Forgive us, inspire us
to make a difference,
to be your willing servants,
become your true disciples
within this fragile world.

God of old year and new,
be with us as we meet
the many challenges,
tasks and opportunities
the coming year will bring,
and grant us strength, joy,
patience and perseverance
as we seek to do your will.

Your disciples
gave up so much
to follow you,
yet we hold on,
not realising
how much
in letting go
we have to gain.
So forgive us
and free us,
to follow daily
and unburdened
to where you lead.

Bless the givers,
eyes open
for those in need
of prayer,
encouragement,
support,
a little time,
the gift of love.
In the act of giving
and receiving
may both be blessed.

Gracious God, forgive
the inconsistencies,
those gaps between
Scripture's words
and our daily lives
into which we fall.
Steady our feet,
strengthen faith,
that our words
might bring blessing
and our actions
reflect your love.

For those who seek
but have yet to find
the road to follow,
may we become
signposts, pointing
beyond ourselves,
to guide them safely
on the well-trodden
but glorious route
to their destination.

In a fractious, divided world,
be the truth that informs us,
the strength that supports us
and the love that inspires us
to be different, imitators
of the one who made us.

Open our hearts and minds
to discern the truth,
or not, in others' words.
And in what *we* say
and do, hold fast to that
we know is true, your Word,
and show that through our lives.

May these eyes reflect your glory
May this mouth sing out your praise
May these hands be used in service
May these feet go where you lead.

Gracious God, may you be found
not only in quietness of prayer,
ocean's edge or mountain peak,
but in the bustle of everyday life;
in children's laughter, conversation,
a beggar's bowl, a busker's song,
market hall or production floor,
sparkling eyes, a smile, a tear,
lover's embrace, high five, a hug,
the struggle of increasing years.
May you be found in pain and joy,
gain and loss, for you are there,
around, within, if we have eyes to see.

Gracious, loving Lord,
as you touch our lives
so hearts are warmed
and burdens eased,
feet are steadied
and faith renewed,
hands made useful
and lives restored,
as you touch our lives,
gracious, loving Lord.

May a song of joy
be in our hearts,
even if the sky
is dark, and life
is hard, and hope
thin on the ground.
And in that song,
that sacrifice,
may hearts be warmed,
eyes lifted high
and faith restored
in One who knows,
and cares, and loves
enough to die
and rise again for us.

Transform our struggles
into victories.
Transform our doubting
into certainty.
Transform our stumbles
into confidence.
Transform our sorrow
into worshipping,
gracious God, we pray.

As we run this race
called life, passing
the baton of faith
one to another,
grant us strength
along the road,
encouragement
and perseverance,
that together we
might cross the line
and claim the prize.

For love that cares less
about where we have been,
and more about where
we could be, we thank you.

Be the wisdom
in my words.
Be the love
in my embrace.
Be the healing
in my hands.
Be the blessing
as we part.

Bless all for whom today
is the departure point
on a journey of faith.
May they find company
and fellowship among
their fellow travellers,
on this now well-walked
though narrow road,
and have confidence
in the one who guides
and leads them safely
to their journey's end.

May we never forget
from where we have come,
the distance travelled
and the love that guided us
to where we are today.
Gracious and patient God,
there with us always,
encouraging, supporting,
our hope and our peace,
accept our grateful praise.

Ever-loving, ever-giving God
be the light that guides our way
and the life that lives within,
be the word that comes to mind
in every moment of despair,
be the eyes that see a need
and the healing in our touch,
ever-loving, ever-giving God.

Gracious God, we thank you
that you can use these lives,
these imperfect lives, to fulfil
your purposes and become
the means through which
others might meet with you
and know your saving grace.
For the faith you have in us
and the roles prepared for us
we offer everything we are,
and everything we can become
through your love and power.

May your love, which has
no preconditions other than
a willingness to be received
be the pattern for our lives
and the seed that we sow,
in a world quick to judge
and yet slow to see a need.

You are the potter, Lord,
and in your skilful hands
even the unlikeliest of clay
becomes a thing of beauty
and useful, bringing glory
not to the pot, but its creator.
So take these lives, this clay,
and in your loving hands
transform and make us
into what we long to be;
made useful, Lord, for you.

Gracious God, increase our faith
and confidence, so when you call
our response is in the knowledge
that you will equip us for tasks
laid out before us, and together
we can sow precious seeds
into soil prepared and waiting,
that will, in your perfect timing,
blossom and produce much fruit.

Bless the sharers
of time, resources,
gifts and kindness,
and all whose lives
will be brightened
by their generosity.

Loving God, in your light we are walking,
in fellowship and strength, together,
sure of the path, less likely to stumble,
supporting each other, growing in faith
and knowledge of you, slowly becoming
the people you are daily calling us to be.

Thank you, Heavenly Father
for the gift of your Word,
handed down by generations
who, through its wisdom,
knowledge and insight
discovered within poem,
letter and prophetic words
the only one who could fill
that 'God-shaped hole'
within their heart and soul,
and passed that knowledge
to others, who did the same
and found their Saviour,
their Father, their brothers
and sisters in your name.
Help us to share our faith,
in our lives and conversations,
that your glorious Word
might be written on hearts
and your Truth and Wisdom
be seen and proclaimed
throughout this beautiful world.

Eternal God, in a world
of conflicting values
you are the only rock
on which to build
that isn't sinking sand.
A solid rock of truth
and a firm foundation
that can withstand
even the fiercest storm.

Sometimes, Lord, those wide roads
with pleasant views seem easier,
more comfortable to walk along
than the one you have set us on.
But though narrow in comparison
there is less to distract us, tempt
or even cause us to lose our way.
This narrow road is made for us,
a waymarked trail, well-trodden
and designed to lead us safely
to a chosen, glorious destination.

Bless the Lord, O my soul,
be still and remember
all the Lord has done;
in our darkness when
his word was our light,
in our gladness when
his joy was our song,
in our weakness when
his touch was our strength,
in our coldness when
his love was our warmth.
Bless the Lord, O my soul,
be still, be still and remember.

Holy Spirit, infuse our lives
with your living presence.
Let that river of peace flow
through these willing hearts,
and your wisdom and grace
be the qualities we display
wherever life may take us.

May we look at others
as if through your eyes;
less judging, more loving
and seeing them, like us,
as not perfect or finished
but as a work in progress
that will be completed
in due time by your hands.

May the little we can offer,
that mustard seed of faith
become, through you, a tree
that can endure life's storms,
stand firm, and in due course
begin to blossom and bear fruit.

This journey is made easier
knowing you're beside us,
for you know this path well,
having walked it before,
and will not let us stumble
if we follow your instruction
and put our trust in you.

Lead us to those quiet places
where we might rest awhile,
listen to your gentle whisper
alongside this world's voices
and, recognising the difference,
pay attention to your word
and live it out in our daily lives.
For in you, dear Lord, we trust.

You lead us from the old,
the baggage of the past that,
in carrying, slowed us down
with its increasing weight,
and invite us to lay down
that burden and walk free
with you into a better place,
where, in the company
of your children we can find
contentment, love and peace.
For this freedom, we rejoice!

Planted in the Word of God
Refreshed by Living Water
Sustained by the Bread of Life
Warmed by the Spirit's flame
May your faith not only grow
But blossom and bear fruit

Give us the courage
to explore the gifts
you have given,
removing from us
the old excuse of
'I couldn't do that...'
and in its place
a new willingness
to explore the person
we could truly be.

Health & Wellbeing

For all who struggle
to cope with change
in the shifting scenes
of life – childhood,
education, families,
identity, relationships,
employment, faith,
growing older, dying -
bring hope, a sense
of your love for them,
a glimpse of eternity.

Bring your peace
into stress-filled
and anxious lives,
that gentle calm
into our busyness.
A moment's rest
to stop, re-focus,
feel your presence,
hear your whisper
and reconnect.

God of wholeness,
heal the hurts,
both inside and out,
that make life
difficult each day.
Ease the pain,
loosen the chains,
bringing freedom
in their place.

Healing God bring your wholeness
into relationships that are hurting.
Not a dressing that will peel away
or a restoration of what once was,
but a process of transformation
where over time wounds can heal,
pain decrease, and lives once more
embrace within your love and grace.

Gracious God, bless those
for whom today is a struggle
through pain, adversity,
loneliness, depression,
poverty or circumstance.
Step into their helplessness
through the compassion
and love of those who care -
be it family, friend, neighbour
or stranger, and your Spirit
bring comfort and wholeness
to both body and soul.

For all whose nights are broken
by pain, discomfort, anxiety,
caring duties, noisy neighbours
and so many other reasons,
leaving them irritable, tired
and unable to concentrate,
refresh their minds, grant
patience in times of stress,
keep them safe when driving,
and in the nights to come
may they find peace and rest.

Gracious God, be with those
whose lives are consumed
by the loving care of others,
and exhaustion leaves them
empty from the act of giving.
Grant them refreshment,
rest, and strength enough
for the challenges of the day,
and may they, and the ones
within their care be blessed,
as love is given, and received.

God of wholeness,
for all whose day
is accompanied
by chronic pain,
pour your Spirit
as a soothing oil,
bringing relief
and freedom
from the chains
which hold them,
and a song of joy
into their hearts.

Give strength to the weary,
whose nights are broken
regularly by the crying
of a child, caring duties,
illness, pain and infirmity,
street noise or anxiety.
Bless them with patience
as they face each day,
and in moments of calm
enable them to rest.

Be close to those who,
growing old, are afraid
of what the future holds.
Grant them the strength
for daily tasks, and more,
a joy of life that can rise
above its aches and pains,
and by your Holy Spirit
become a daily blessing
to all who they shall meet.

Gracious God be with those
who, through lack of rest,
begin most days exhausted.
Keep them safe at work
and calm their anxieties.
In moments of tension
grant them peace,
and at the end of the day
bring them safely home
and bless them with sleep.

Bless all who face change
or uncertainty in their lives,
whether through changes
in well-being, relationships,
employment or location.
May they find strength,
peace and encouragement
for the challenges ahead,
and sense your presence
with them on this journey.

Loving God, we pray for those
who, through unexpected loss
find their lives torn apart by grief.
Wrap your arms around them,
let them feel your warmth fill
the emptiness within their hearts,
hear your gentle whisper
reassuring them of your love
and, in those closest to them
find the strength to carry on.

In winter's long, dark days
be with all who are lonely,
frail, depressed, housebound.
Loving God, may they sense
your presence - the calmness
and comfort of your Spirit -
with them through this day,
lifting their spirits, bringing
hope of brighter days ahead.

Gracious God, we bring to you
those regular aches and pains
that greet us every morning
and have become a part of us.
Today we bring them to you,
and, hands outstretched, ask
for healing, and your Spirit
to flow in and through bone,
muscle and sinew, bringing
freedom, wholeness and peace.

Struggles Along the Way

For all who struggle
to find their identity
in a world that tries,
often without success,
to find a suitable box
in which to place them,
grant them courage
to become the people
you want them to be,
not constrained
by this world's wisdom
but allowed to grow
and become themselves
in your Spirit's power.

Bless all whose journey,
that search for faith,
acceptance and identity,
is made more difficult
by circumstance, doubt,
diversions, exhaustion,
stumbles along the road
and the load they carry.
May they hear your voice
and see your footsteps,
know how close you are,
lay down their burden,
reach for your hand
and allow you to lead them
into their promised land.

Wherever believers struggle
to declare their faith openly
without risking prosecution,
keep them safe, and if words
cannot be spoken, may lives
speak of your gracious love
and this, your unspoken truth,
touch both mind and soul
as your gentle Spirit flows
from one heart to another.

Bless the strugglers
on faith's journey
who, slowed down
by all they carry,
still persevere
and won't give up.
Grant them strength
and opportunity
to let go, and leave
behind those things
no longer needed.
And in that release
may they discover
the grace and love
they are searching for.

May you find comfort
in the knowledge that
even in your weakness
God's grace is sufficient,
his love surrounding,
his Spirit within, giving
strength for each day.

For all who feel less loved,
less wanted, discriminated
against within the country
they have known as home,
draw close, precious Jesus,
you who, facing rejection
still loved the very ones
who called for you to die.
Draw close, embrace them,
remind them of their worth
and that you gave your life
so they might know your love.

Gracious Lord, clear away
all the debris we carry
that is slowing us down,
impeding our progress.
All the hurts and failures,
prejudice and faults
preventing us becoming
the people we could be.
We lay them before you.
Free us from these chains
so we can run with you,
and live again the life
that we were created for.

May your voice be heard,
a sharp blade cutting
through the wisdom
of a world that struggles
to separate truth from lies.
May your voice be heard,
not just from pulpits
but on factory floors
where potential prophets
await your Spirit's empowering.
May your voice be heard
and spread abroad
by those who recognise
the need for change,
for hearts and minds
to be renewed.

Comfort the bereaved,
be with them in their loss
and fill their emptiness
not only with the love
and compassion of friends,
but also with your peace,
and the firm conviction
that those we have lost
may have departed this life
but remain in your loving care.

Forgive our frustration, Lord,
when this world does not turn
in the way we would like it to.
Grant us humility to realise
change comes from within.
Help us examine, and change
if necessary, the way we think
and act, sowing a few seeds
within our day that might just
take root, grow and blossom,
making this a more beautiful
and sustainable world for all.

Nearly always, Lord, it is when
we give up trying, come to you
on bended knee and in humility
confess our need, that we find
what we have been looking for,
discover the faith that until now
we lacked, and in that moment
of revelation find healing, peace
and by your grace, forgiveness.
For such love and patience, Lord,
we offer our unending thanks.

God's peace be your anchor
through the storms of life,
a solid rock to hold on to
until gales have ceased.

Bless the children who,
because of background
or circumstance, do not
fulfil their true potential
in our education system,
and are disadvantaged
from such a very early age.
Forgive us if we are guilty
of not doing enough
to support the vulnerable,
the neglected, and those
who have already given up.
Give wisdom to teachers,
support workers, parents
and all who desire the best
for all our nation's children,
that they might not only
survive, but go on to thrive.

Help all those raising children,
and struggling to understand
the pressures that they face
in their journey into adulthood.
Help us to guide them safely
through what seems at times
uncharted waters, your wisdom
the rock upon which we stand
to assist them on their way.
May they reach their destination
safely, your love sustaining
and enriching their daily lives,
which may in turn become
a blessing to parents, guardians
and carers everywhere we pray.

Too often, Lord, we excuse
our little indiscretions,
harsh words and actions,
and move on, hoping
they might go unnoticed,
or worse, not caring at all.
Forgive us, transform us,
show us your better way
so we might live each day
sowing your love and grace
within this beautiful, fragile Earth.

Bless the strugglers;
the slow to keep up,
happier to stay put
sheep within your flock.
Lead them gently
from where they are,
and from valley floor
to higher ground,
where they might see
beyond the small
if comfortable world
they currently inhabit,
to a different place of
green pastures, still water
prepared for them by you.
Lead them, Gentle Shepherd,
to where they need to be.

Breath of God
bring life into
these dry bones

There are many questions
about this world to which
we struggle to find answers,
so, Lord, we are here again
seeking wisdom, insight
into situations that worry,
anger or cause anxiety
to so many people today.
Open our ears to listen
and our voices to proclaim
your word, that truth
this world so needs to hear

Forgive us, Lord,
when we see
and do not act,
when we hear
but do not speak.
A moment gone,
opportunity
for our hands
and voices
to be yours,
bringing grace
and healing
into this world.
Forgive us, Lord.

Break down the hardness
in our hearts, Lord,
the wall that insulates
us from the world,
the wall that stops us
feeling others' pain.
Break down the hardness
in our hearts, Lord,
so we might see and touch
this world with your love,
and through grace
transform its pain to joy.

When the day ahead
is a mountain to climb
or wilderness to cross
and we are ill-prepared,
may faith and strength
be increased so that,
properly equipped,
and with you as guide,
we find that our destination
no longer seem so distant.

Lord, you have said
that to truly love you
then I must also
love my neighbour,
which can be difficult
when we disagree
or lifestyles clash.
Yet in overcoming
those difficulties
it is possible to see
the miracle that you
love someone like me.
Teach us to love, Lord,
as you have loved us
that this world might be
a better neighbourhood
in which to live and share.

Lord God, you are our refuge
in times of trouble, help
when storm clouds gather,
strength in our weakness,
peace within our busyness,
the focus of our worship,
our confidence and hope.

When I am afraid
I put my trust in you.
When life hems me in
and I have no time
or space to think,
I put my trust in you.
When people's words
leave painful scars that
never seem to fade,
I put my trust in you.
When body's weak,
and even simple tasks
take far too long,
I put my trust in you.
In God, whose word
I praise – in God I trust
and am not afraid.

(based on Psalm 56:3,4)

For Light in Darkness

Be present Lord, wherever kids
grow up believing that gangs
give them identity, family,
belonging, protection, power,
and find themselves drawn
into an often-dangerous world
that robs them of childhood,
leaves scars difficult to heal.
Bless those called to work
with these young people,
sharing your unconditional love
with both word and lives.
Protect and empower them
as they invite these prodigal sons
and daughters into your family.

In a world of fake news,
lies and half-truths,
may this be known,
your word is true
and everlasting,
Your word is love
and brings healing,
your word is joy
to those searching,
your word is hope
to those struggling,
your word unites
rather than dividing.
In this fragile world
in which we live,
Lord God, may it be
your word that we trust.

Amid each day's confusing news
Lord, may your words be heard,
and our ears discern the difference
between this world's truth and yours

Bring light into the dark world
of young people growing up
in a culture of gangs and drugs,
with lives controlled by fear.
Bless those who work within
those streets, befriending,
engaging, breaking chains
enslaving so many children.
Keep them safe, these sowers
of hope for a better future,
working in such barren soil.
May it be watered by your Spirit,
and in due time, produce much fruit.

God of peace, breath on this fractured world
and heal the divisions that grow daily wider.
Breathe on leaders, that they might respect
the right of all human beings to live in peace.
Breathe on those who hate, opening the hand
clenched in a fist, that it might embrace.
Breathe on the influential, that their power
might be used for the common good of all.
Breathe on the individual, and bring freedom
from conflict, and a life that's free from fear.
God of peace, breath on this fractured world.

Gracious God, be with those
forced to leave their homes
through fear of strong winds
and flooding, afraid of loss,
disruption, the potential cost.
Keep safe the vulnerable,
the emergency services,
and all working to ensure
law and order is maintained.

Merciful God, help this world,
consumed as it is with greed,
arrogance and self-interest,
to realise that those outside -
the poor, homeless, outcast,
exploited and marginalised -
are our equals in your eyes,
and as brothers and sisters
equally deserving of our care.
Let us not forget to whom
your love and healing touch
brought such transformation,
the hungry, blind, lost and lame,
and look for opportunities
to do likewise in your name.

Breathe peace into this world,
to dispel the heated rhetoric
and divisive words that serve
only to fan the flames of hate.
Breathe peace into cold hearts,
as a warming breeze to waken
the seed of love that sits inside,
waiting to germinate and grow.
Breathe peace into this world.

Open the ears of the many
longing to hear your voice
who, deafened by the world,
have yet to hear you speak.
Bring them to a quiet place
where they can be at peace
and, in a moment's stillness,
let them hear your words
of comfort, love and grace,
so that, in days that follow,
they may discern your call
through this world's noise
and know that you are close.

Bless those whose joy
is to give of themselves
in the offering of time,
patience, advocacy,
comfort and kindness
to someone in need.
May they, in giving
be filled with your love
such that, overflowing,
they may never run dry!

Be known Lord, in the hearts
of those for whom street gangs
are family, and acts of violence
rites of passage; young people
immune to the consequences
of their actions on another's life.
Be there Lord, in their midst,
speaking both to heart and mind,
and flush hatred from their lives,
sowing seeds of love and grace
that may, in your good time, flower.

Rid our hearts of attitudes
that do more harm than good;
the cynicism, self-interest,
envy, anger and falsehood
that are mis-shaping
the political landscape
and seeping into daily life,
causing division between
nations and neighbourhoods.
Let your ways be known,
your love proclaimed
and this world transformed,
for the glory of your name.

May all those who have power;
business, economic or political,
use it, not for their own benefit,
but for the common good of all,
that this world might be a fairer,
and more equitable place to live,
where you might look one day
and find your love alive and well,
in the hearts of all your children.

Bring a blessing into the lives
of young people who are,
through circumstances
well beyond their control,
now the principle carer
for a family member,
and whose childhood
and education is on hold
whilst, with loving care
and devotion, they do
the very best they can.
Lighten their load, Lord,
give time for them to play.
Bring light into their darkness,
a song of joy into their souls.

Creator God, there is no mystery
to the question 'Why are we here?'
It is to be witnesses to the beauty
of this universe and the world
on which we live and breathe.
And, in caring for this garden
that we might pass it on, entire
and not damaged to our children,
this precious, priceless gift from you.

May we be seekers after
and speakers of the truth,
in a world that increasingly
is forgetting its importance

In an often divisive world
where religious voices
invoke your name
to justify so much
that is unjustifiable,
help us remember
we are all your children -
banker or beggar,
homeowner or refugee,
overweight or underfed,
newly born or growing old -
and your love extends to all,
as indeed should ours.
May our voices and our lives
express nothing that divides,
but simply shares your love
so graciously poured down for us.

Bless the helpers and carers,
who spend their days giving
in so many ways; with family,
local community, homeless,
wherever people are in need.
May their selfless acts inspire
and encourage us all to share
your love, given so generously
that it might be freely spent
and lives both helped and blessed.

In your upside-down world, Lord,
it is not the loudest, most pushy,
media-savvy or self-seeking
who are exalted in your eyes,
but those who are happy to serve;
the humble in spirit, obedient
to your call, glimmers of light
in a troubled and unequal world.
May that be us, Lord, your servants
changing this world in a different
but better and more glorious way.

Light-giving God,
we give you thanks
that even through
the darkest day
your light cannot
be extinguished
within our lives;
a spark remains
to be rekindled,
and you will shine
again in hearts,
minds and souls.
Darkness comes,
but has never
overcome your light.

Ever-present God,
we face this day
emboldened,
in the knowledge
that with you
walking beside us
so much is possible.

Bless those who have,
over many years,
given their all for you,
taken up their cross
and carried it
through green fields
and wilderness,
wherever you have led,
and by their example
inspired others
to leave self behind
and journey too.
Bless them, and all
whose lives they touch,
these, your faithful
and wonderful saints.

The Bigger Picture

In a world of inequality,
of haves and have-nots,
it is good to remember
Lord, in your kingdom
all are of equal worth.
Help us work together
that this might become
a fairer, more equitable
world, reflecting values
of selflessness and love,
where hungry are fed,
the homeless find rest
and no one is worthless
who is loved by you.

Where the values of this world
are those of God let us rejoice,
but let us not become imitators
of anything that considers self
above God and others or seeks
to value human wisdom above
that of the Divine. Rather let us
walk faithfully, willing disciples
imitating only the life of our Lord.

(3 John 1:11)

God of love and justice
speak into the hearts
of all whose words
encourage others
into acts of violence,
and innocent lives
are lost or broken.
Soften their hearts
and open their eyes,
that they might see
your image reflected
in the faces of all people
and know that all
are equal in your sight.

Re-energise your Church, Lord,
that we might worship not only
in song and prayer but in our lives,
and this world begin to recognise
within and through us the love
and life they seek, and enquire
where they might find its source.

Bless the lives of those
we pass this morning
who are heading home
from places of work.
Doctors and nurses,
cleaners and carers,
factory operators,
maintenance workers,
emergency services,
retail shelf-stackers,
long distance drivers.
Those whose hard work
makes our lives easier -
the often forgotten people.
Bless them, and give them
the rest they deserve.

God bless the weary traveller
who has walked so many paths
in the search to find a place
where they can be at peace.
Be with them in their travelling
and as guide, reveal yourself
so that, on this Emmaus Road,
their wandering might cease.

Creator God, forgive us
if we think this world
is simply to be exploited.
Open our eyes to see
the damage that we do.
Open our ears to hear
and not ignore the signs.
Open hearts to change.
Make us the gardeners
and caretakers that you
created us to be,
that this fragile world
might be handed on
with pride, not shame,
to future generations.

For all who see Christmas
as pressure to spend
what they do not have
on things they do not need
and fall deeper into debt,
lead them to wise choices
in their preparations,
that allow the family
to enjoy the season
but also share together
the priceless gift of love,
which is the reason
for this celebration.

For refugees
fleeing poverty,
persecution,
warfare, strife;
seeking freedom,
sanctuary,
a better life.
Keep them safe
as they travel,
and compassion
be a gift they find
at journey's end.

For all suffering grief and loss
through extremes of weather,
be it sunshine, wind or rain;
in their suffering bring comfort,
and blessing through the help
of others, so that individuals,
families and neighbourhoods
might find peace and restoration
from sorrow, pain and despair.

Remembering the saints
of our past, whose lives
inspired us to continue
on our journey, whose
words encouraged us
through green fields
and barren places,
who were shepherds
for a while, and now
reside in pastures new
as your faithful servants
in this life and hereafter,
for whom we give our thanks.

For all those brave voices
speaking out on injustice,
inequality, abuse of power,
and corporate greed, who
want to leave this world
a better, more equitable
place for their children
and grandchildren to inherit.
Who are willing to stand
in the firing line of politics
and suffer the consequences
for speaking out the truth.
Bless their endeavours.
May their voices be heard,
and this world, your gift to us,
begin once more to resemble
the world that you intended.

For all who suffer daily
for the faith they proclaim,
grant them courage
and strength for the fight.
May their witness become
a lamp in the darkness
and a seed that will grow
even in such parched earth,
so that their faithfulness
might extend your kingdom,
and your glory be seen
in every corner of this world.

Gracious God, be close
to all who are victims
of violence and hatred,
exploitation or abuse,
the persecuted people
of whatever faith,
wherever they live,
who are your children,
our sisters and brothers
in your family on earth.
Be close to them, Lord,
and hold them in your arms.

Keep safe the vulnerable
in our towns and cities;
the no-fixed-abode,
rough sleeping,
cold and hungry,
enslaved and exploited,
depressed, suicidal,
the elderly, lonely
and almost invisible.
Bless those who help
with food and clothing,
shelter and counselling.
Increase our awareness
and concern for their needs,
these, your vulnerable children.

May this be a kinder,
more generous world,
less obsessed with self,
meeting others' needs,
considering the future
handed to our children,
being more responsible
in our role as stewards
of this very beautiful
but fragile gift from you.

We pray for justice
wherever people
are traded for profit,
and lives are lost,
abused and scarred.
We pray for victims
and their families,
often deceived by lies,
seeking a future,
not seeing the cost.
Heavenly Father,
for those who mourn
we ask for comfort,
for those who suffer
we ask for healing,
for those found guilty
may justice prevail.

For all those left grieving,
struggling to rebuild lives
after natural disasters -
hurricanes, earthquakes
mudslides and tsunamis.
Bring love and compassion
from government, agencies,
doctors, nurses and all those
willing to be used wherever
the need seems to be greatest.
Bless those who freely give
of time and skills in situations
such as this. May their sacrifice
bring hope to those whose lives
have been so devastated.

May lives be measured
not by the standards
of this world, subject
to change and fashion,
but by those of God,
shown visibly in love,
kindness, self-control
and humility, that bring
a blessing into the lives
of both giver and receiver.

Loving God, this fragile world
cries out, and is ignored.
We are Earth's custodians,
entrusted with its care,
and we have been reckless,
more concerned with self
and what we can extract,
than what might be left
to pass on to our children
and to theirs. Forgive us,
renew our sense of purpose,
and may each one of us
play our part in making this
world a more fitting legacy.
To the glory of your name.

We pray for our children
growing up in a fast-moving
and unpredictable world.
Give them hope and vision,
and may they develop into
your change-makers, working
for the common good of all,
caring for this world, ensuring
a future for those who follow,
as was always your intention.

Brothers, sisters,
mothers, fathers,
sleepers, wakers,
carers, sharers,
drivers, walkers,
drifters, workers,
beggars, bankers,
vendors, spenders,
movers, shakers
helpers, healers,
and many others
we pass today.
Bless them all!

Help us once again
become stewards
and not abusers
of this precious
and fragile earth,
entrusted to us
so we might thrive,
now spoilt for gain
and at such a cost.
Forgive and help us
Creator God, we pray.

Just Being Thankful

May joy be found
in little things -
a smile, a word,
a pleasant stroll,
birdsong, laughter,
flowers, sunshine,
in giving and
receiving gifts,
and for ourselves
a little treat,
time with family,
and space to rest.
In little things
may joy be found.

For the gift of music,
and all who sing, play,
arrange, compose
and touch our hearts
with such emotion,
we give grateful thanks.
For those folk songs
crying out for justice
and hymns of worship
lifting up our souls,
for pop music speaking
to each generation
and symphonies and operas
transcending the years,
we give grateful thanks,
creative and Creator God

Bread of Life, you feed us
with your living word,
and by your Spirit satisfy
the hunger in our soul.

For love that does not see
the worst in us, but rather
the person we could be,
and then, if we allow,
enables us to understand
and realise our true potential,
we offer our grateful thanks.

For the simple knowledge
that you love me as I am,
despite my imperfections,
and from this raw material
can create something new
that will bring glory to you,
I offer my grateful thanks.

For the gift of music,
to move us, soothe us,
excite us, lift us up
or bring us gently
to our knees;
for such a precious
and creative gift,
Loving God, thank you.

Loving God, it is not easy
to see your hand at work
in the everyday of life;
in the places and faces
I pass in my journeying.
Yet beneath the surface
prayers are being said
and conversations had
that will, in good time,
bring change and healing,
light into the darkness.
And so I pray, and trust,
and continue, day by day
to place this beautiful,
troubled, fragile world
into your gentle hands.
We live by faith, not sight.

A song of praise be on my heart
from the moment I am woken,
and later, lying down to rest
may that song remain unbroken

We believe, Lord,
that you live in us
and we live in you,
through the Spirit
and by your grace.
And knowing this
deep in our souls
gives us comfort,
joy and strength
for the day ahead.

For the love you have shown us
as sometimes reluctant disciples,
your patience in being with us
when we decide to go our way,
your hand that is there for us
as we stumble or are anxious,
your gentle whisper reminding us
that you will never let us go,
for all of this and more besides
what can we do but offer you
the worship of our hearts and lives.

Clear our minds
of all that hurts
ourselves and others,
and in the space
a song of joy,
a word of praise,
a smile, a hug,
sharing your love,
the simple things
that make this world
a better place

If I were a composer, Lord,
I'd write a graceful symphony
and fill a concert hall with praise.
If I were an artist, Lord,
I'd paint a vibrant altarpiece
to bring alive a church's prayer.
But here I stand before you, Lord,
no baton or paintbrush in hand,
simply offering all I am, for you.

Your Spirit leads us
along faith's journey
and we are happy
to follow this, your path,
at a comfortable pace.
But now and then, Lord,
your Spirit dances,
and though it is for joy
we find it difficult
keeping to the rhythm
and stumble as we try.
It's lack of practice, Lord,
so please, teach us to dance,
that worship might become
as natural as walking
in our journeying with you.

(Galatians 5:25)

For the many little things
that cause us to be different,
that sum up our uniqueness,
Creator God, we thank you

Today, shall we make
a fashion statement,
be bolder in choosing
the clothes we wear.
Let's choose Humility,
Kindness, Gentleness
Compassion, Patience.
Brands such as these
don't go out of fashion,
and make a statement
about their Creator
that words alone can't do.

As the gentle breeze
encourages branches
and leaves to move
to this world's rhythm,
may your Spirit's breath
touch heart and soul,
and cause this body
to move to your beat!

Lord God, the more we know you,
the more we see how lives
are transformed by your presence,
not just in those times of crisis
when we're down on our knees,
but in the ordinary moments,
the getting-on-with-life moments
when you put a song into our hearts
that lifts that cloud of tiredness,
or bring to mind a word of yours
that somehow was just needed.
Lord God, the more we know you,
the more often we find ourselves
quietly saying; 'Thank you.

Blessing

God's Spirit empower you
God's freedom release you
God's wisdom direct you
God's justice inform you
God's mercy inspire you
God's love be seen in you
and change this world through you

God bless your travelling;
quiet whisper to guide you,
strong hand to support you,
soft rain to refresh you,
warm sun to restore you,
God's love to sustain you

God's love be in your word and action
God's grace be in the song you sing
God's joy be in your contemplation
God's peace be in your journeying

God's arms around you
God's love within you
God's word inspiring you
God's light guiding you
Journey in peace today

God's peace be with us,
lifting our anxieties,
lightening our step,
restoring vision,
filling hearts with hope

About the Author

John Birch is a Methodist Local Preacher and writer living in South Wales, and has a website www.faithandworship.com which is a well-used resource of prayer and Bible study material.

Also available in paperback are *Ripples – engaging with the world in prayer, Prayers of Life,* and *Fragrant Offering*, a Celtic-inspired Liturgy.

Follow the author on his Faith and Worship Facebook page where new prayers are shared throughout the week.

Printed in Poland
by Amazon Fulfillment
Poland Sp. z o.o., Wrocław